BEHIND THE CURTAIN

Act Out History

STRUCK GOLD

CALIFORNIA GOLD RUSH

Virginia Loh-Hagan

45TH PARALLEL PRESS

Published in the United States of America by Cherry Lake Publishing
Ann Arbor, Michigan
www.cherrylakepublishing.com

Reading Adviser: Marla Conn, MS, Ed., Literacy specialist, Read-Ability Inc.
Cover Designer: Felicia Macheske

Photo Credits: © Flugklick/Shutterstock.com, cover, 1; © Everett Historical/Shutterstock.com, 5, 11, 21, 23, 25; © Library of Congress, LC-USZ62-25376, 6; © optimarc/Shutterstock.com, 12, 29; © Library of Congress, LC-DIG-pga-05072, 17; © chippix/Shutterstock.com, 18

Graphic Elements Throughout: © Chipmunk131/Shutterstock.com; © Nowik Sylwia/Shutterstock.com; © Andrey_Popov/Shutterstock.com; © NadzeyaShanchuk/Shutterstock.com; © KathyGold/Shutterstock.com; © Black creator/Shutterstock.com; © Edvard Molnar/Shutterstock.com; © Elenadesign/Shutterstock.com; © estherpoon/Shutterstock.com

45th Parallel Press is an imprint of Cherry Lake Publishing.

Library of Congress Cataloging-in-Publication Data

Names: Loh-Hagan, Virginia, author.
Title: Struck gold : California Gold Rush / Virginia Loh-Hagan.
Description: Ann Arbor : Cherry Lake Publishing, [2020]. | Series: Behind the Curtain | Includes index.
Identifiers: LCCN 2019032891 (print) | LCCN 2019032892 (ebook) | ISBN 9781534159426 (hardcover) | ISBN 9781534161726 (paperback) | ISBN 9781534160576 (pdf) | ISBN 9781534162877 (ebook)
Subjects: LCSH: California–Gold discoveries–Juvenile literature. | California–History–1846-1850–Juvenile literature.
Classification: LCC F865 .L83 2020 (print) | LCC F865 (ebook) | DDC 979.4/04–dc23
LC record available at https://lccn.loc.gov/2019032891
LC ebook record available at https://lccn.loc.gov/2019032892

Cherry Lake Publishing would like to acknowledge the work of the Partnership for 21st Century Learning, a Network of Battelle for Kids. Please visit *http://www.battelleforkids.org/networks/p21* for more information.

Printed in the United States of America
Corporate Graphics

A Note on Dramatic Retellings

Participating in Readers Theater, or dramatic retellings, can greatly improve reading skills, especially fluency. The books in the **BEHIND THE CURTAIN** series give readers opportunities to learn about important historical events in a fun and engaging way. These books serve as a bridge to more complex texts. All the characters are real figures from history; however, their stories have been fictionalized. To learn more about the people and the events, check out the Viewpoints and Perspectives series and the Perspectives Library series, as the **BEHIND THE CURTAIN** books are aligned to these stories.

TABLE of CONTENTS

HISTORICAL BACKGROUND

James Marshall was a carpenter. He was working at Sutter's Mill. Sutter's Mill is in California. He was hired to build a **sawmill** powered by water. While working, he found gold flakes in the river. This happened in 1848.

Gold was discovered! News spread. The California Gold Rush began. Thousands of **miners** rushed to California. They wanted to find gold. They wanted to strike it rich.

Most people came in 1849. These miners were called "the '49ers." They borrowed money. They left their homes. They left their families. They traveled to California. They crossed mountains. They sailed across seas. Some miners traveled from Latin America, Europe, Australia, and China.

FLASH FACT!

James Marshall was the first person to discover gold at Sutter's Mill.

Vocabulary

sawmill (SAW-mil) a factory that saws logs into lumber

miners (MINE-urz) people who work underground and dig tunnels to get minerals like gold and coal

FLASH FACT!

San Francisco, California, grew rapidly in 1848 and 1849.

Vocabulary

claims (KLAYMZ) areas that are staked out for mining

equipment (ih-KWIP-muhnt) gear and tools

boomtowns (BOOM-tounz) towns that popped up and thrived

Miners staked out **claims**. Mining was hard work. Miners had to move rock. They had to dig. They had to walk in freezing streams. Some miners lost fingers. Some got sick. Some died. **Equipment** was expensive. Living conditions were tough. Times were dangerous. People looted. They shot each other.

The peak of the gold rush was in 1852. About $2 billion worth of precious metals were found. Over 750,000 pounds (340,194 kilograms) of gold was found. California grew a lot. About 300,000 people came to California. Mining camps were set up. They became **boomtowns**. California became an important place. It entered the United States as the 31st state.

CAST of CHARACTERS

NARRATOR: person who helps tell the story

JOSEPH MARKS: a former soldier who gets a job as a builder at Sutter's Mill

JENNIE WIMMER: a cook who works at Sutter's Mill

CHARLES HAYWARD: a former schoolteacher from New York who rushed to California in 1849 as a gold **prospector**

MIRANDA HAYWARD: wife of Charles Hayward

MARIO FERNANDEZ: a miner from Chile who rushed to California as a gold prospector

BACKSTORY
SPOTLIGHT BIOGRAPHY

Luzena Wilson lived from 1819 to 1902. She was born in North Carolina. She moved to Missouri. She got married and had 2 children. She heard about the gold. She rushed to California in 1849. Her journey was tough. While traveling, she'd make dinner for her family. A miner came up to her. He gave her money for one of her biscuits. Wilson saw a business deal. She was smart. She cooked meals. Miners paid in gold. They wanted a home-cooked meal. Wilson used this to her benefit. She opened a hotel in Sacramento, California. The hotel got flooded. She moved to Nevada City. She opened another hotel. She made a lot of money. A fire burned down her Nevada City hotel. Wilson moved. She bought land in Vacaville and helped build it into a town. In 1877, she moved to San Francisco.

Vocabulary

prospector (PRAHS-pekt-ur)
someone looking for minerals in the ground

FLASH FACT!

Peter Burnett was the first elected governor of California. He served during the gold rush.

ACT 1

NARRATOR: JOSEPH MARKS *is working at Sutter's Mill. It's 1848. He's eating dinner. He's talking to* **JENNIE WIMMER***.*

JOSEPH: We're so lucky to have you cook our meals. The men around here can't cook.

JENNIE: There aren't many women here. Most jobs are for men. So, I'm thankful for the work.

JOSEPH: It's nice to be able to eat good food after a long day of **manual** labor.

JENNIE: So, what brings you to California?

JOSEPH: I needed the work as well. I was a soldier in the war against Mexico. We won, and I had nowhere to go. I was already here in California. I heard John Sutter was building a sawmill. Sutter needed strong, **able** men. So, I signed up!

Vocabulary

manual (MAN-yoo-uhl) physical work

able (AY-buhl) having the ability to do something

FLASH FACT!

In mining areas, the population of women was under 2 percent.

NARRATOR: *It's January 24, 1848. There's a lot of excitement at Sutter's Mill.* **JOSEPH MARKS** *rushes to* **JENNIE WIMMER**.

JOSEPH: Mr. Marshall, our boss, may have discovered gold!

JENNIE: Really? Tell me more!

JOSEPH: Mr. Marshall saw a **gleam** in the river. He picked it up.

JENNIE: What did it look like?

JOSEPH: It looked like yellow flakes. It sparkled in the sun. Another worker pounded the flake on a flat rock. It didn't break. So, we think it might be gold.

JENNIE: Bring me a piece. I can test to see if it's gold.

JOSEPH: How do you do that?

JENNIE: I'll throw it into my **kettle**. I put it with my soap mixture. If it's gold, it'll stay **intact**. If it's not gold, it'll melt into the soap.

Vocabulary

gleam (GLEEM) bright shine

kettle (KET-uhl) cooking pot

intact (in-TAKT) together

FLASH FACT!

People mistook fool's gold for real gold.

NARRATOR: **JENNIE WIMMER** *confirmed it was gold! News spread. It's now 1849.* **CHARLES HAYWARD** *and* **MIRANDA HAYWARD** *are in New York. They read about the gold at Sutter's Mill.*

CHARLES: Here's another **article** about the gold in California.

MIRANDA: So many people are getting rich quick.

CHARLES: Maybe we should try our luck? We could use the money. I don't get paid that much as a teacher.

MIRANDA: I heard people go to California and come back with at least $10,000 in gold. It's worth a try.

CHARLES: When do you want to leave?

MIRANDA: I can't go with you. Our children are too young. It's too dangerous.

CHARLES: You and the children can stay with my brother. I'll share my gold with him when I return.

LOCATION SHOOTING

REAL-WORLD SETTING

John Sutter was a Swiss immigrant. He got a land grant in the Sacramento Valley. He got 50,000 acres (20,234 hectares). He got it from the Mexican government. His land was at the point at which the American River flowed into the Sacramento River. He used the land to create farms. He named it New Switzerland. This happened in 1839. Today, the land is Sacramento. At the center of his land, he created his headquarters, Fort Sutter. Today, Fort Sutter is a national historic site. It was where James Marshall showed Sutter the gold. This discovery brought many gold rushers to his land, bringing on the start of the California Gold Rush.

Vocabulary
article (AHR-tih-kuhl)
news report

FLASH FACT!

Pamphlets spread the news of California's gold rush.

NARRATOR: CHARLES HAYWARD *travels to California. He meets* **MARIO FERNANDEZ** *at Sutter's Mill.*

CHARLES: Are you here for the gold as well?

MARIO: Yes. I heard a man can get rich with just a few days' work. I'm here to try my luck.

CHARLES: Me too!

MARIO: Where did you come from?

Vocabulary

steamer (STEEM-ur)
a ship powered by
a steam engine

FLASH FACT!

Posters advertised passage aboard ships to the California gold region.

CHARLES: I came from New York. I took a **steamer** to Chicago. Then, I traveled in wagons over land. What about you?

MARIO: I came from Chile. I traveled by ship. I landed in San Francisco. Then, I came here.

CHARLES: You're lucky that you didn't have to travel by wagons.

MARIO: Why? Was it tough?

CHARLES: It wasn't easy. We traveled through the desert in Nevada. There was so much dust. Sometimes, the dust choked me. I saw broken wagons. I saw animal **corpses**.

MARIO: How was it when you got to California?

CHARLES: We traveled through the mountains. It was dark. There was snow and ice. Some of the people who traveled with me went back home. Some got sick. Some died. I felt like quitting too. But I kept thinking of my family.

MARIO: Well, tomorrow is our first day at the gold site. Let's hope we get lucky!

Vocabulary
corpses (KORPS-iz)
dead bodies

FLASH FACT!

Prospectors traveled over rough and wild land to reach California.

ACT 2

NARRATOR: **CHARLES HAYWARD** *and* **MARIO FERNANDEZ** *are at Sutter's Mill. They're eating dinner.* **JENNIE WIMMER** *is serving them.*

JENNIE: Any luck today?

CHARLES: Not yet.

JENNIE: Keep at it. Lots of people are here. You never know!

MARIO: Any luck for you, Charles?

CHARLES: Not for me. I've been busy. I helped my team build a **dam**. We wanted to lead the river waters away from the best spots to find gold. But I'm not even sure how to find gold.

MARIO: I can help you. I know how to dig mine **shafts**. I also know how to **pan** for gold. If there's not enough water, dry wash sand to find gold flakes.

CHARLES: How do I do that?

Vocabulary

dam (DAM) an obstacle designed for blocking water

shafts (SHAFT) long narrow passages that lead down into something

pan (PAN) to shake a pan back and forth to see if gold falls to the bottom

FLASH FACT!

Miners used different methods to find gold.

MARIO: Fill a large bowl with sand. Toss everything into the air. Do this over and over again. Blow on it as the sand falls. Catch it in the bowl. Do this until only gold is left.

CHARLES: What are some other ways to find gold?

MARIO: You can use a **corvo** to pick gold from cracks in the rocks. You can use a **poruna** to test sand for gold.

CHARLES: How do you know so much about finding gold?

MARIO: My father and grandfather were gold miners.

CHARLES: That's great. Thank you for teaching me.

NARRATOR: ***JOSEPH MARKS** and **MARIO FERNANDEZ** are panning for gold in the same place. Years have passed. It is 1852.*

MARIO: You're out here late.

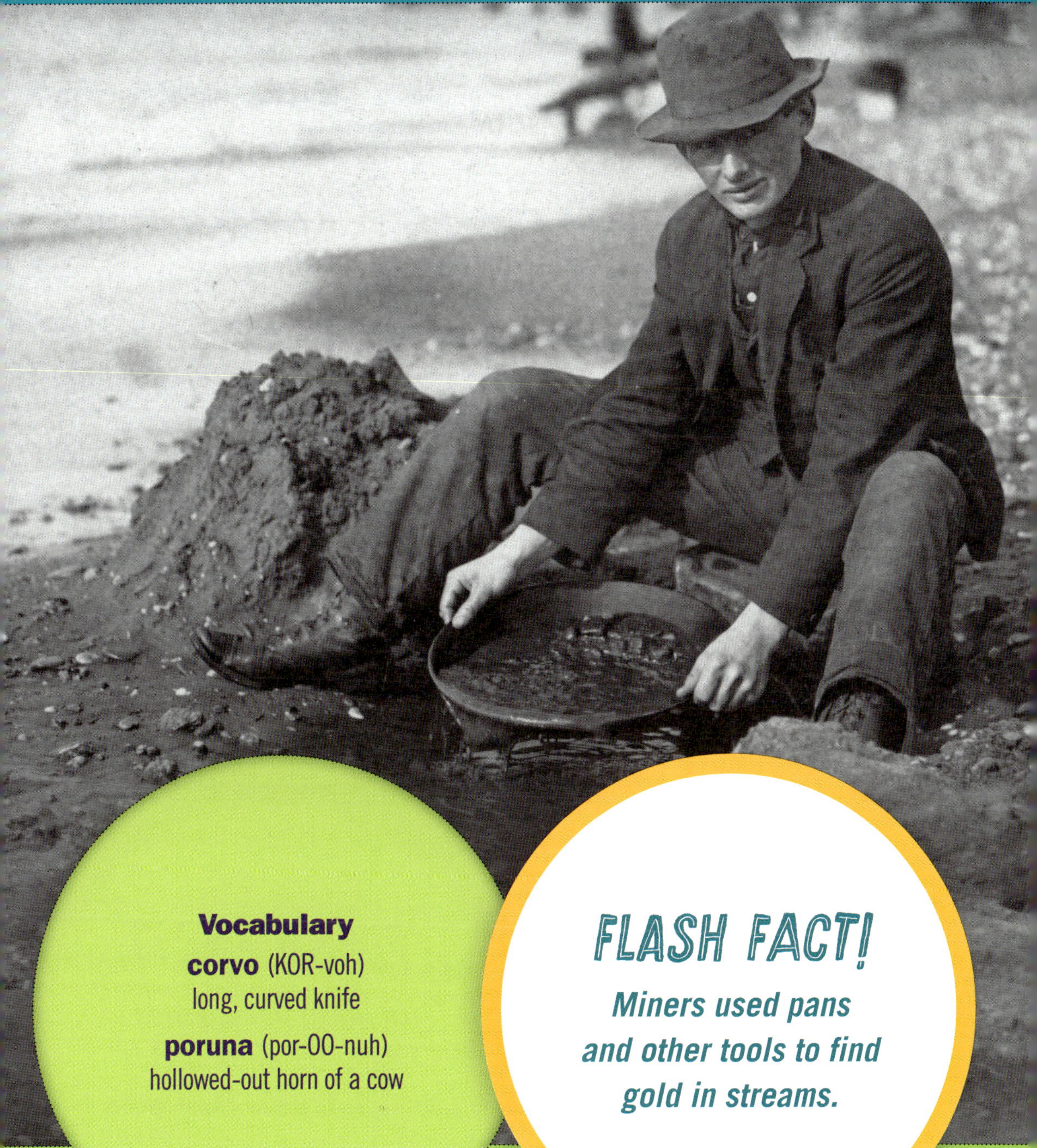

Vocabulary

corvo (KOR-voh)
long, curved knife

poruna (por-OO-nuh)
hollowed-out horn of a cow

FLASH FACT!

Miners used pans and other tools to find gold in streams.

JOSEPH: I got hired to build the sawmill. So, I can only pan for gold during my free time. What about you?

MARIO: It's easier to work at night. Some people don't want us here.

JOSEPH: What do you mean?

MARIO: Some of the Americans don't like having **foreign** miners here. The government is charging us a special tax. A gang is robbing us. They beat us up. They make us pay money for protection.

Vocabulary
foreign (FOR-uhn)
from a different country

FLASH FACT!

Chinese miners also came to California for the gold rush. They were treated unfairly.

JOSEPH: That sounds awful. You are being treated so unfairly.

MARIO: It's not right. I don't think I can take much more. I'm thinking of going back to Chile.

JOSEPH: What are you going to do there?

MARIO: I've made enough money here. I can set up a hotel. I can open a store. And, best of all, I'll be home!

JOSEPH: That sounds great. I'm also thinking about packing it up.

MARIO: What are you going to do?

JOSEPH: I have my **wages** from building the sawmill. I found a few bits of gold. I'll go to San Francisco. I've always wanted to open up my own store.

MARIO: We may not have struck it rich. But we are a part of history.

JOSEPH: Yes! We were here at the birth of the California Gold Rush. We saw it all happen!

NARRATOR: **JENNIE WIMMER** *and* **CHARLES HAYWARD** *are talking over dinner.*

BLOOPERS

HISTORICAL MISTAKES

Some Chinese immigrants worked as laundrymen. Chinese laundrymen looked inside the miners' clothes. They found gold bits. They shook gold dust from miners' clothes. There's a story about a Chinese immigrant named John John. John John worked in Weaverville, California. He didn't charge for doing laundry. Miners called him a "laughingstock." But the joke was on them. John John was smart. He collected gold from their clothes. He rinsed out the gold. He scrubbed the clothes clean of gold. He became rich. Chinese immigrants weren't treated fairly. They took whatever jobs they could. Many became cooks, servants, and laundrymen. Chinese immigrants helped improve mining. For example, they introduced the water wheel to wash gold.

Vocabulary

wages (WAYJ-iz)
payment for work

FLASH FACT!

Some miners stayed in California. They settled where they mined. They built log cabins.

JENNIE: I hear you're going home soon.

CHARLES: I miss my family so much. Being away from them makes me appreciate them more.

JENNIE: I'm sure they miss you too. How much gold did you find? Are you going back home a rich man?

CHARLES: I have about $500 worth of gold dust.

JENNIE: It's too bad not everyone can strike it rich here. Some people are just luckier than others.

CHARLES: My dream of hitting the **mother lode** didn't happen. But I am rich with adventures. I traveled out West. I panned for gold. I've had enough excitement for a lifetime.

Vocabulary

mother lode (MUHTH-ur LOHD)
a main source of gold or silver

FLASH FACT!

Some of the miners' wives stayed home. They took over the family businesses.

EVENT TIMELINE

- **January 24, 1848:** James Marshall discovers gold at Sutter's Mill. John Sutter visits the site. He wants to keep the gold a secret for a while. But word gets out.
- **February 2, 1848:** The Treaty of Guadalupe Hidalgo is signed. This ends the Mexican-American War. California becomes a U.S. territory.
- **March 15, 1848:** A San Francisco newspaper reports there's gold in California. The first miners head to California.
- **May 12, 1848:** Sam Brannan shows off some gold. He runs through the streets in San Francisco. He yells, "Gold, gold, gold from American River!" He inspires men in San Francisco to head to gold mines. Gold fever hits San Francisco. Brannan's store sells equipment for miners. He makes a lot of money.
- **August 19, 1848:** The *New York Herald* reports about the gold. It's the first eastern newspaper to do so.
- **December 5, 1848:** President James K. Polk makes a speech to Congress. He confirms the gold in California. People rush to California.
- **April 1849:** About 30,000 men meet in Independence, Missouri. They travel in wagon trains to California.
- **April 1849:** The first American gold rushers to sail for California arrive in San Francisco. They had to sail around Cape Horn.
- **April 1850:** California passes the Foreign Miners Tax. This law charges foreign miners each month. They have to pay in order to work claims. The tax is repealed on March 14, 1851.
- **September 9, 1850:** Congress agrees to the Compromise of 1850. This admits California into the United States.
- **May 1852:** The Foreign Miners Tax is passed again. It targets Chinese miners.
- **1852:** There are crop failures in China. Chinese people leave China. Over 20,000 Chinese immigrants arrive in San Francisco.
- **1850–1855:** Gold at the surface is mostly gone. Miners have to dig deeper to find gold. New technology is developed to do this.

CONSIDER THIS!

TAKE A POSITION! Imagine you live in the 1850s. You just heard about the California Gold Rush. Would you move to California? Would you try your luck? Is it a good idea? Argue your point with reasons and evidence.

SAY WHAT? Read the 45th Parallel Press book about Angel Island. Explain how Angel Island and the California Gold Rush are connected.

THINK ABOUT IT! People went to California to strike it rich. They were hoping to change their fortunes. What would you do if you found gold? How would you spend your money?

Learn More

Hall, Brianna. *Strike It Rich! The Story of the California Gold Rush.* North Mankato, MN: Capstone Press, 2015.

Holub, Joan. *What Was the Gold Rush?* New York, NY: Grosset & Dunlap, 2013.

Lusted, Marcia Amidon. *The California Gold Rush.* Ann Arbor, MI: Cherry Lake Publishing, 2015.

INDEX

ABOUT THE AUTHOR

Dr. Virginia Loh-Hagan is an author, university professor, and former classroom teacher. When she taught fourth grade, she loved teaching about the gold rush! She lives in San Diego with her very tall husband and very naughty dogs. To learn more about her, visit www.virginialoh.com.